Solids and liquids

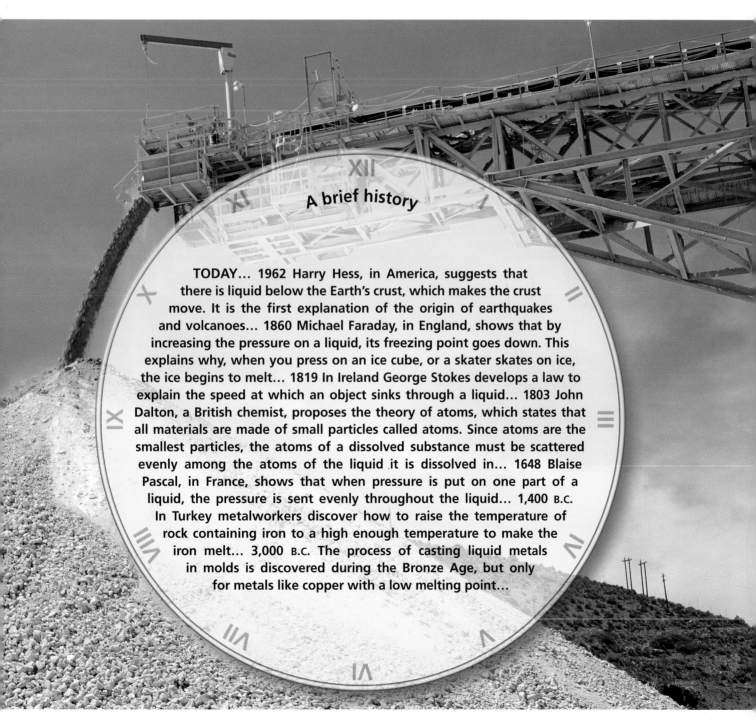

A brief history

TODAY... 1962 Harry Hess, in America, suggests that there is liquid below the Earth's crust, which makes the crust move. It is the first explanation of the origin of earthquakes and volcanoes... 1860 Michael Faraday, in England, shows that by increasing the pressure on a liquid, its freezing point goes down. This explains why, when you press on an ice cube, or a skater skates on ice, the ice begins to melt... 1819 In Ireland George Stokes develops a law to explain the speed at which an object sinks through a liquid... 1803 John Dalton, a British chemist, proposes the theory of atoms, which states that all materials are made of small particles called atoms. Since atoms are the smallest particles, the atoms of a dissolved substance must be scattered evenly among the atoms of the liquid it is dissolved in... 1648 Blaise Pascal, in France, shows that when pressure is put on one part of a liquid, the pressure is sent evenly throughout the liquid... 1,400 B.C. In Turkey metalworkers discover how to raise the temperature of rock containing iron to a high enough temperature to make the iron melt... 3,000 B.C. The process of casting liquid metals in molds is discovered during the Bronze Age, but only for metals like copper with a low melting point...

Dr. Brian Knapp

Word list

These are some science words that you should look out for as you go through the book. They are shown using CAPITAL letters.

CONTRACT
To shrink. The opposite of expand.

CRYSTAL
A solid that has a regular shape, like a cube, with flat faces meeting at sharp angles.

DENSE
The weight of something compared to the amount of space it takes up. For example, oil is less dense than water, and so it floats on water.

DISSOLVE
To break up into tiny particles within a liquid.

EXPAND
To swell. The opposite of contract.

FLEXIBLE
Something that will bend or stretch easily without breaking.

FORCE
Anything that pushes or pulls on an object. Forces include pressure, gravity, and magnetism.

GEMSTONE
A crystal that people believe to be especially beautiful and so valuable. Diamonds and rubies are examples of gemstones.

GRAIN
A small, hard particle. It refers to things from the size of sand up to the size of grains of wheat.

INSOLUBLE
A substance that will not dissolve at all in a particular liquid.

LANDSLIDE
A very rapid sliding or flowing of wet soil or similar material down a steep slope. Landslides usually begin without warning. They usually only occur when the material is full of water, such as after heavy rain.

LAVA
The liquid material that flows from a volcano during an eruption.

LIQUID
A form of a substance in which the particles are free to move around but are still loosely touching one another.

MINERAL
A solid that consists of just one substance. Emerald is a mineral because it is all made of the same thing.

MIXTURE
A combination of two or more substances that have become stirred together.

MOLTEN
A substance that has changed from a solid to a liquid.

PARTICLES
Pieces of a substance that are too small to be seen except with special microscopes. They are much smaller than dust.

POWDER
A ground-up solid.

SOLID
A form of a substance in which the particles are attached together. As a result, a solid keeps a fixed shape unless it is pushed or pulled.

SOLUBLE
A substance that will dissolve in a particular liquid.

SOLUTION
A mixture of a liquid with another liquid, a solid, or a gas.

SUSPEND, SUSPENDED
To keep particles of a solid temporarily from settling out of a liquid by keeping the liquid moving.

VOLUME
The amount of space that a substance takes up.

Contents

What is a solid?

A SOLID is made up of very tiny PARTICLES that hold together very strongly.

What do these have in common: a metal coin, a metal gear box, a tub of margarine, a clay animal, paper, and wool?

The answer is they are all solids (Picture 1). A solid is any substance that cannot change shape freely. You may be able to push or pull it into a new shape (as when you scrape over the margarine with a knife, make wood fiber into paper, or make a fleece into wool). But once put in that new shape, it will not change by itself.

Clay animal

Metal coin

▲▼ (Picture 1) These materials are different in many ways, but they are all solids.

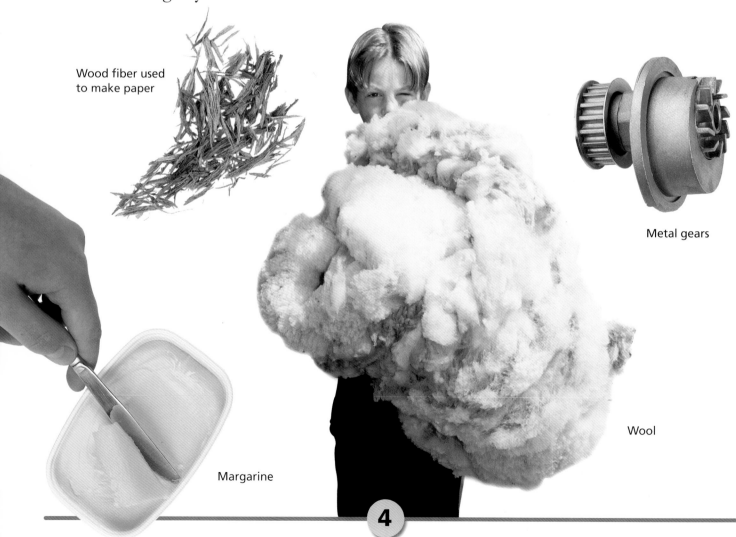

Wood fiber used to make paper

Metal gears

Wool

Margarine

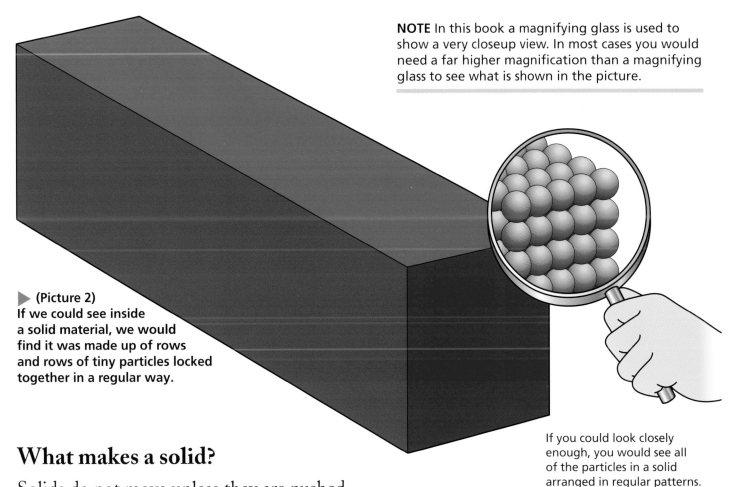

NOTE In this book a magnifying glass is used to show a very closeup view. In most cases you would need a far higher magnification than a magnifying glass to see what is shown in the picture.

▶ **(Picture 2)**
If we could see inside a solid material, we would find it was made up of rows and rows of tiny particles locked together in a regular way.

If you could look closely enough, you would see all of the particles in a solid arranged in regular patterns.

What makes a solid?

Solids do not move unless they are pushed or pulled because they are made of tiny particles that are stuck tightly together (Picture 2).

Why some solids are flexible

You can change the shape of some solids just by pushing or pulling them. These solids are FLEXIBLE. When you push or pull a flexible solid, you unstick some of the particles it is made from. That allows the particles to slide past one another. Once you stop trying to change its shape, the particles stick back firmly together again.

How solids change

When you warm a solid, its shape can be changed more easily. For example, when butter comes out of the fridge, it is a hard block, but in a warm room it soon becomes softer. When steel is heated in a furnace, it becomes softer and can more easily be squashed or beaten into a new shape. Both soft and hard forms of these materials are still solids because, until they are FORCED into a new shape, they will not change shape on their own.

Summary
- A solid keeps a fixed shape unless it is pushed or pulled into a new shape.
- Most solids are hard and strong, but some are soft and flexible.

Crystals

CRYSTALS show us how solids are made of particles packed in a regular way.

One of the most beautiful natural shapes is a snowflake (Picture 1). Snowflakes are made of many ice crystals locked together. If we look at a single snowflake, we find it is made with six points. There are many shapes of snowflake, but they always have six points.

If you were able to look really closely at a snowflake, you would find that it is made of tiny particles of ice all locked together in a regular way. The particles can only lock together one way, and that is why snowflakes always have six points.

This is what a single snowflake looks like.

◀▲ (Picture 1) A snowflake is a regular shape because it is made of ice crystals locked together in a regular way.

To get the crystals in a snowflake to form, they have to have room to grow. That usually happens when liquids turn into solids very, very slowly. Water turns into ice very slowly high in clouds.

Salt and sugar crystals

All crystals are made of particles locked together in regular ways. You can see examples of crystals in your kitchen. Look closely at sugar grains or sea salt. These crystals are in the shape of cubes (Picture 2).

Sulfur crystals

▼ (Picture 2) These are grains of sea salt. Each grain is a cube. If you were able to look at the salt very closely, you would find that it is made up of box-shaped particles locked together. It does not matter what size the salt grain is, it will always be a cube.

▲▼ (Picture 3) Crystals have flat faces that reflect the light. When you look at the flat face of a crystal, you are looking at the natural way the particles are arranged. The crystals above are yellow sulfur. Look at the shiny surfaces. They tell you that the material is a crystal.

The most famous crystals are gemstones, like diamond and ruby, but even pure metals form crystals.

Crystals all have regular shapes, such as a cube. The crystal below is a cube of a mineral called pyrite, which contains iron.

Gemstones

Some of the most beautiful crystals in the world also formed very slowly from liquids. They are called **GEMSTONES**. Gemstones form deep in the Earth, in places where the rock is **MOLTEN**. When the molten rock begins to cool, crystals start to form.

It takes millions of years for fantastic crystal gemstones to form (Picture 3).

Diamonds, emeralds, rubies, and similar substances (called **MINERALS**) are all crystals, each with their own special shape.

A pyrite crystal

Summary
- Crystals are solids that have grown in a regular way.
- Crystals often grow in liquids as they cool.
- Crystals have flat, shiny surfaces.

Grains and powders

GRAINS and POWDERS are small pieces of solid. Because they are small, both grains and powders can move more easily.

You may think of solids as being large chunks of material that do not move—the bricks in a wall, for example. But pieces of solids move quite easily (Picture 1) even when they are quite large.

The smaller the material, the easier it moves. Think, for example, of the grains of sand on a beach or grains of rice or wheat. Some particles of solid are even smaller. They make powders, like flour, for example.

How solids move

If you have ever tried piling up dry sand or rice grains, you found that you can never make the pile at a very steep angle (Picture 2). That is because the grains don't stick together very well. As a result, grains and powders *appear* to pour like a LIQUID.

The effect of water

Water has an important effect on grains and powders. When grains or powders are damp, the water sticks them together. That is why you can make a sandcastle out of the damp sand on a beach, but you cannot make a sandcastle in a sandpit of dry sand.

▼ (Picture 1) When solid pieces are small, they look as though they are being poured. Even quite large pieces behave this way when they move. In this waste pile the conveyor is adding fist-sized pieces, which then roll down the sides. Notice how, when solids are "poured," they build up into a cone. The ash that falls during a volcanic eruption also rolls down the side of some volcanoes and helps explain their conical shape.

▶ (Picture 2) When sand moves, as in this antique hour-glass, it pours through a hole and forms a cone-shaped pile in the bottom glass. Although the sand appears to flow as it passes through the hole, we know it is made of grains. If it were a liquid, it would take the same shape as the bottom of the hour-glass.

The ingredients for a cake that you mix in a bowl behave the same way. The flour and sugar are loose and easy to move around when they are dry (Picture 3). But as soon as water or milk is added, they stick together and form a dough. However, if you add too much liquid, all of the strength of the solids is lost.

▼ (Picture 3) These pictures show what happens when cake ingredients are mixed with different amounts of water.

A

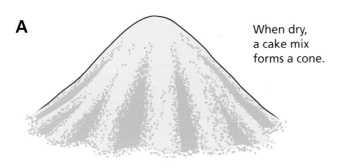

When dry, a cake mix forms a cone.

B When milk or water is added, the ingredients are made damp, and they form a strong dough.

C

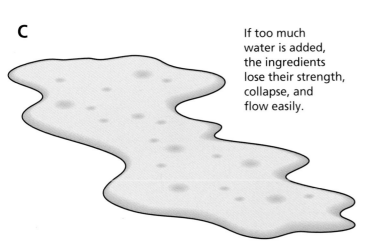

If too much water is added, the ingredients lose their strength, collapse, and flow easily.

Soils and landslides

Soils are made of small particles. Just like a cake mix, soil will hold together best when it is damp. However, when a soil gets very wet, it loses its strength and can easily flow. When this happens, it can cause a **LANDSLIDE**.

Landslides can be extremely dangerous. In 1966, for example, there was a mound of coal waste high on a hill overlooking the village of Aberfan in Great Britain (Picture 4). The coal waste was made of small pieces, just like a soil. When it became full of water from a nearby spring, the coal simply flowed down the hillside and straight into a primary school. Within seconds 144 children and their teachers were killed.

▼ (Picture 4) The tragedy of Aberfan, Great Britain, happened because the spaces between grains of coal waste became full of water.

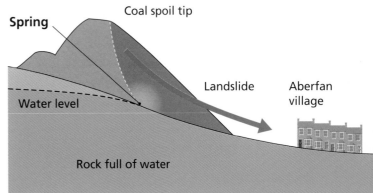

Coal spoil tip

Spring

Landslide

Aberfan village

Water level

Rock full of water

Summary
• Grains and powders are small particles of a solid.
• Dry powders and grains can move easily.
• Damp grains and powders hold together.

What is a liquid?

LIQUIDS have no strength of their own and take the shape of the container that holds them.

Heat a solid, and it turns into a liquid; cool a liquid, and it turns into a solid. That can happen because the solid and liquid forms of a material are both still made of the same substance. The difference between a solid and a liquid is only the way the particles of the material are held together.

In a solid like a candle the particles are all held firmly together. In the liquid form of candle wax the particles have become unstuck. Although they are still always touching one another, they are free to move around and drip (Picture 1).

Liquids have no fixed shape

A liquid has less strength than a solid and so will not stay in any shape on its own. When a liquid flows into a container, it takes up the shape of the container, filling it from the bottom up (Picture 2). The top surface of the liquid is always level.

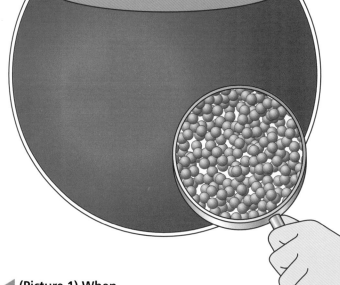

If you could look closely enough, you would see the particles in a liquid touch, but they are *not* arranged in a regular pattern.

◀ **(Picture 1) When a candle is heated, it melts and drips onto the paper, then becomes a solid again.**

▲ **(Picture 2) A liquid always takes on the shape of the container it is put in.**

If you tilt the container, the liquid flows until its top surface is level again (Picture 3). If it is poured from one container to another, it will take up the shape of the new container. If a liquid is poured onto a table, it will spread out all over the table because there is nothing to contain it.

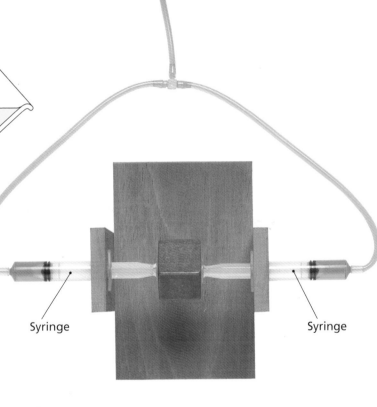

▼ (Picture 3) The top surface of a liquid remains level even if the container is tilted.

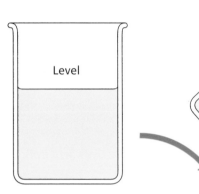
Level

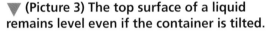
Level

Syringe

Syringe

Syringe

Liquids do not squash

Although a liquid easily changes shape, it can't be squashed because all of the particles are still touching.

You can see this very clearly in Picture 4. In this experiment two syringes are holding a wooden block. A third syringe is used to made a piston. When the piston is pushed in, the liquid in the third syringe is squeezed down the connecting tubes, and the pistons in the other syringes are pushed out. This can only happen because the liquid can move easily, but it cannot be squashed.

▲ (Picture 4) You cannot squash a liquid, so if you press down on it, the pressure goes through the liquid. That is the principle at work above. Car brakes work in much the same way.

Summary
- A liquid always takes up the same amount of space (it does not change its volume).
- A liquid does not have a fixed shape but changes shape easily (it pours).
- A liquid cannot be squashed.

Runny liquids

Some liquids are runnier than others, but most can be made more runny by being warmed.

All liquids are runny, but some liquids are more runny than others.

To test this, you could pour out different liquids and see how fast they spread. But there is a less messy and better test. To try it, fill one clear, tall container with water, and fill another identical container with cooking oil.

If you drop a marble into each of the containers at the same time, you can easily see which sinks fastest (Picture 1).

If you fill a third jar with cooking oil and then put it in the fridge for a few hours, you can test whether the cold oil is stickier than the oil kept at room temperature. You will see that a marble sinks more slowly in cold oil than in warm oil.

Some liquids become much stickier when they are cold and much runnier when they are warmed. You have seen that oil is one of them.

Why some liquids are runnier when warm

When some liquids are cold, their particles grip together more strongly, and so the liquid changes shape more slowly. When these kinds of liquids are warm, their particles only grip weakly, and so the liquid becomes runnier.

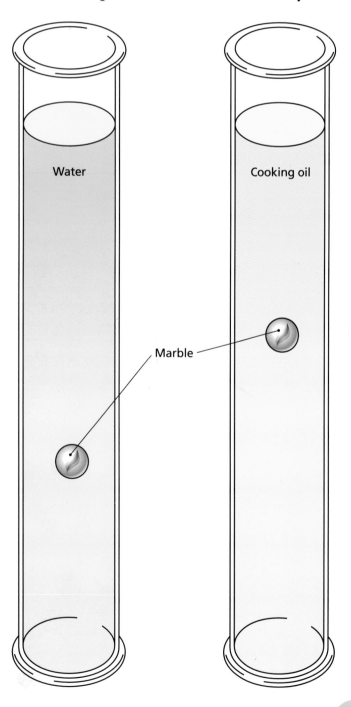

Water

Cooking oil

Marble

◀ (Picture 1) Two containers, one filled with water (left), and the other filled with cooking oil (right), can be used to show that water is runnier than cooking oil.

▲ (Picture 2) This is lava erupting from a volcano. It is so hot and runny that it makes a waterfall.

Lava on the move

LAVA is a natural material that comes from deep under the ground when a volcano erupts. When the lava first comes out of the ground, its temperature is over 1,000°C.

When lava first flows from the volcano, it is runny and makes fountains, flows in rivers, and even pours down over ledges to make fiery waterfalls (Picture 2). But the longer it flows, the cooler it gets, and so the stickier it becomes.

As the lava becomes cooler, it slows down. You can see it cooling down because it changes color from red to black (Picture 3). Once it is cool, the lava is so sticky that it can move no further, and so it stops. It has turned into a solid.

▲ (Picture 3) When lava has traveled over the land for some kilometers, it hardly moves forward at all. Finally, it cools to a black rock.

Summary

- Some liquids are runnier than others.
- Some liquids become more runny when they are warmed.
- Some liquids become stickier as they cool.

Hot liquids rise, cold liquids sink

When a liquid becomes warm, it gets lighter and rises; when it cools, it becomes heavier and sinks.

Cold water flows to the heater

Hot water rises

When a liquid warms up, it swells; and when it gets cold, it shrinks. When the liquid swells, each particle takes up more space, but the total number of particles does not change. We say the liquid is now lighter, or less **DENSE**. Once it is lighter, the liquid rises just as a float bobs up to the surface of a pond.

The opposite happens when a liquid cools. The particles in a cool liquid take up less space, and so it tends to sink.

Hot water rises

When a hot liquid rises, other, cooler liquid flows in to take its place. You

▲ (Picture 1) The purple dye in this tank shows what happens when water is heated. The warmed water is less dense, and so it rises, then spreads out over the surface. As water rises above the heater, other colder water is pulled in to take its place. The process is called convection.

can clearly see how this happens when a heater is placed at the bottom of a tank (Picture 1). A purple dye has been used to show what is happening. As water over the heater is warmed it becomes less dense and rises. Cold water flows in and is heated in turn. That sets up a kind of natural stirring motion.

The same happens when you heat a saucepan of water. The water at the bottom of the pan gets hot and rises to the surface, while colder water sinks down to take its place.

Cold water sinks

If ice is placed in a drink, it floats on the surface. The ice cools the water next to it. As the water becomes colder, it becomes more dense and sinks to the bottom of the glass, pushing warmer water back to the surface (Picture 2). This kind of stirring is much slower than heating because an ice cube is not very cold, but a stove gets very hot.

When water doesn't move

Warmed water naturally rises above cold water. So, if you heat water at the surface, it will stay on the surface and will not mix easily with the cold water below it. The same thing happens in lakes and oceans. The water on the surface is warmed by the Sun, but the deeper water stays cold.

The fact that hot water stays above cold can be put to good use. In your hot-water tank at home (Picture 3) the water is always drawn off from the top because that is the hottest part of the tank. The hot water doesn't mix with the cold water entering at the bottom.

Ice cube

◀ (Picture 2) The purple dye shows the way that water moves when it is cooled. The ice cube floating on the surface cools the water, which then sinks down the outside of the glass.

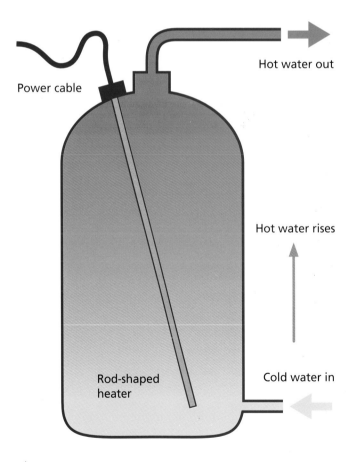

Power cable

Hot water out

Hot water rises

Cold water in

Rod-shaped heater

▲ (Picture 3) In a hot water tank hot water is taken from the top, and more cold water flows in from below. This means that you draw off all of the hot water before you draw off any cold.

Summary
- If liquids are warmed from below, they rise.
- If liquids are cooled at the top, they sink.
- If liquids are cooled at the bottom or heated at the top, no movement takes place.

Swelling and shrinking

Both solids and liquids change in size as they become hotter and colder.

Straw

Cork or rubber stopper

Water

Thermometer

If you have ever looked at a thermometer, you will see that it contains a fine tube partly filled with liquid. As the temperature rises, the liquid swells and also rises in the tube. In this way the swelling of the liquid measures the temperature.

All liquids will change in size, or **VOLUME**, as they change temperature. A simple thermometer can be made from a glass (not thin plastic) bottle completely filled with water and sealed with a tightly fitting stopper that has a straw through it (Picture 1). As the temperature rises, the water swells, or **EXPANDS**, and begins to move up the straw. As the temperature falls, the water shrinks, or **CONTRACTS**, and the level of the liquid falls.

Making use of expansion

All solids expand when they get warmer and contract when they cool. Blacksmiths and other craftsmen made

▶ **(Picture 1) A real thermometer inside a bottle thermometer. Both show how liquids swell as they get warmer and shrink as they cool.**

use of this property for hundreds of years. In the past, when they needed a tightly fitting iron rim on a wooden wheel, for example, they would heat up the wheel rim until the iron was red hot. By this time it would have expanded enough to slip onto the wooden rim. Once the rim was in place, the iron would be drenched with water, cooling it down so that it shrank, gripping the rim firmly.

Expansion rates

Every substance expands or contracts by a unique amount as its temperature changes. In general, metals shrink and swell more than other solids.

Some thermometers make use of this fact (Picture 2).

Most liquids shrink and swell much more than any solid. Water will swell, for example, very much faster than glass. That is why a liquid can be used in a thermometer tube.

However you need to be careful when heating liquids and solids. If you heated a full bottle of liquid with its stopper firmly in place, the liquid would try to swell more than the glass of the bottle, and that could eventually make the bottle burst.

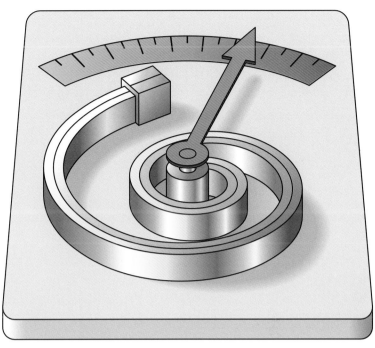

◀▲ **(Picture 2)** This thermometer uses strips of two different metals bound together. They are shaped into a spiral, and a pointer is attached to one end. The other end is fixed. When the temperature rises, the metals expand; and when the temperature falls, the metals contract. These changes cause the needle to move.

Summary

- Both solids and liquids shrink when they get colder.
- Both solids and liquids swell when they get hotter.
- Every substance expands and contracts at its own rate.

Mixtures

When you mix some materials together, they do not change, and so you can sometimes separate them again.

There are many kinds of **MIXTURES**. You can mix solids, like powders or soil; you can mix liquids, like water and orange juice; and you can mix solids and liquids, like sugar in water.

Mixing solids

If you make a cup of coffee, you might begin by mixing a spoonful of instant coffee granules with a spoonful of sugar (Picture 1). If you make a cake, you might first mix flour and sugar.

All that has happened is that the particles of coffee and the sugar, or of flour and sugar, have got jumbled up. But if we wanted to take the trouble, we could eventually separate the sugar from the coffee or the flour again.

You can mix things up in any proportion you choose: three parts of coffee and two parts of sugar or ten parts of sugar and one part of flour.

Whatever you do, it will still be possible —if very difficult—to separate all of the ingredients.

Mixing liquids

If you stir two liquids together, you also get a mixture—it is called a **SOLUTION**.

In a solution one of the substances seems to have disappeared completely into the other one. When this happens, we say that one substance has **DISSOLVED** in another substance. You cannot see two separate liquids any more.

But actually, nothing has changed. When one substance dissolves in another, it spreads out so evenly in the solution that the particles are too small to see (Picture 2). But the particles of the two substances are still separate.

▼ (Picture 1) A mixture of coffee granules (brown) and sugar (white) show that when solids are mixed, they are simply jumbled up. It doesn't matter what the proportions are.

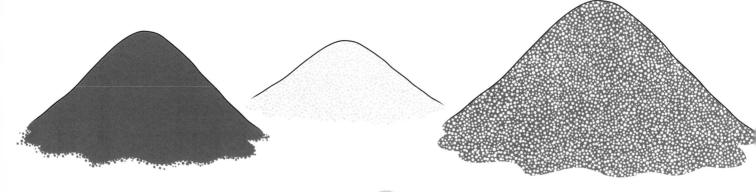

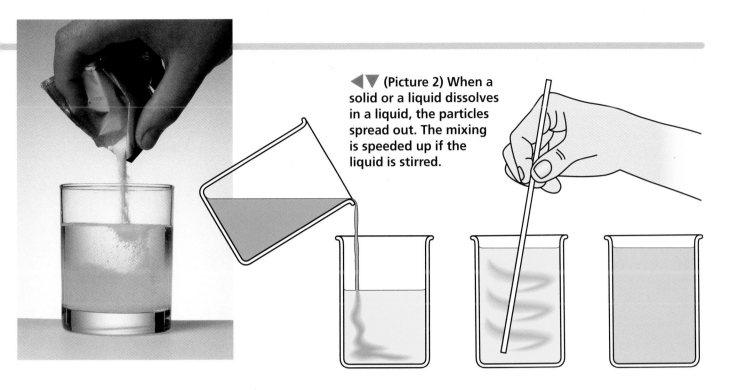

(Picture 2) When a solid or a liquid dissolves in a liquid, the particles spread out. The mixing is speeded up if the liquid is stirred.

Mixing solids and liquids

Many solids dissolve in liquids to form a solution. If you watch grains of coffee, food dye, or another colored substance dissolve in water, you can see what happens (Picture 3). Particles of the solid substance, such as the coffee, are attracted to the water. First, all of the surface particles are attracted away. That exposes new particles to the water, and they are then attracted away, too. As this happens, the particles in the water start to move away, spreading out evenly in the water. Each particle is too small to see, but we know they are still there because they give the water a new color.

However, you can't keep pouring more and more liquids or solids into liquids. There is a limit to how much a liquid can dissolve. Beyond this limit no amount of stirring will help, and the remainder will settle at the bottom of the container.

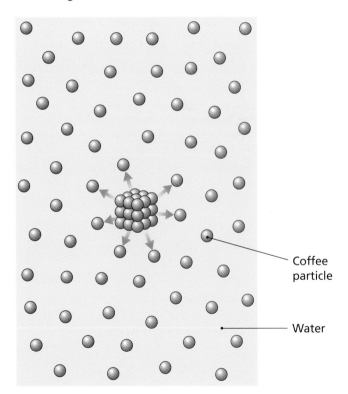

(Picture 3) What happens when a coffee granule dissolves in water.

Coffee particle

Water

Summary
- Solids can be mixed together in any proportions.
- There is a limit to how much of a solid or a liquid can be dissolved in another liquid.
- Solids or liquids that won't dissolve will stay unmixed at the bottom of the container.

19

Soluble and insoluble

Some liquids and solids seem to disappear in other liquids. They are called SOLUBLE substances. Not all substances are soluble.

You can add some liquid or solid to some liquids, and they will disappear and leave the liquid clear. We call this disappearing act "dissolving." For example, we say that salt dissolves in water. Liquids or solids that dissolve in a liquid are called soluble.

But even though the salt seems to have disappeared, the salt and water are still a mixture, as we saw on page 18.

Why we use solutions

Solutions are very important for carrying materials to where they are needed. A liquid fertilizer, for example, is a way of dissolving a chemical in water so that it can be washed into the soil. Most of the materials from our food are carried around our bodies in a solution—blood (Picture 1).

Not all solids dissolve

If you put soil in water, the soil will settle out at the bottom of the container. It will not dissolve (Picture 2). A material that does not dissolve is called an INSOLUBLE material.

If the insoluble material is very tiny, it may stay mixed up in the liquid for a long time, and so it may appear to dissolve. Milk, for example, is made of tiny fat globules spread out in water. They have not dissolved, which is why the cream eventually separates out, leaving a watery substance below (Picture 3). Paint is another material in which the solids (in this case a powder of tiny colored particles) have not dissolved in the liquid. Most food does not dissolve in water.

▼ (Picture 1) Blood is a solution of an almost colorless watery liquid and many different solids, including the red blood cells that give blood its color.

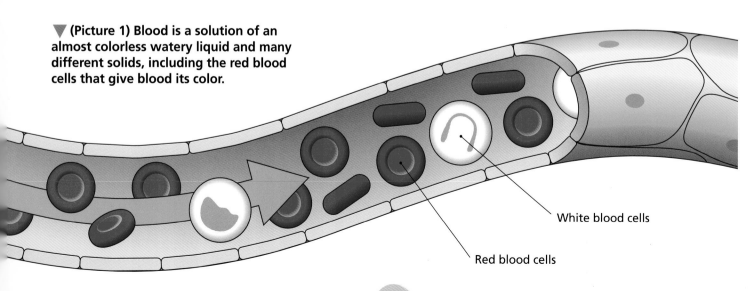

White blood cells

Red blood cells

Which liquids dissolve substances best?

Many liquids dissolve other substances, but the most common one is water. More substances dissolve in water than any other liquid.

However, there are many common substances that do not dissolve in water. Peas and carrots, for example, do not dissolve in the water they are cooked in.

Metals do not dissolve in water, nor does pottery or glass. That is why we can use these materials as containers to hold water.

Other common substances that do not dissolve in water include greasy substances. That is why you have to use a special chemical (dish powder) when you want to wash greasy dishes.

Summary
- Not all substances dissolve.
- Some insoluble materials take a long time to settle out.
- Water dissolves more substances than any other liquid.

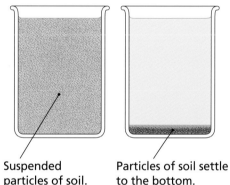

▶ (Picture 2) Particles of soil are insoluble in water. If you stir soil in water, the swirling water will make the particles stay SUSPENDED for a while, but then they will settle to the bottom, leaving the water clear.

Suspended particles of soil.

Particles of soil settle to the bottom.

▼ (Picture 3) Milk contains fat that does not dissolve. When milk is left to stand, the fat rises to the surface as cream. (In "homogenized" milk a special process breaks the fat down into such small pieces that it takes a very long time to separate from the liquid.)

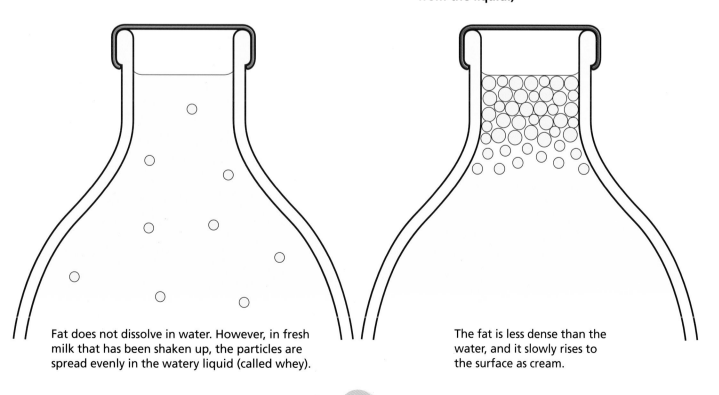

Fat does not dissolve in water. However, in fresh milk that has been shaken up, the particles are spread evenly in the watery liquid (called whey).

The fat is less dense than the water, and it slowly rises to the surface as cream.

Separating mixtures

It is possible to separate mixtures into the substances that make them up. Some are easier to separate than others.

It is easy to mix two substances together, but much harder to separate them.

Separating different sizes

Sometimes you may have a whole range of materials of different sizes all mixed up together. A dry soil, for example, contains stones and sand as well as fine powder called clay.

One way to separate stones from sand and clay is to use a sieve (Picture 1). It is a tray whose bottom is made of a mesh of crisscrossing wires. The larger the number of wires, the smaller the holes between the wires, and the smaller the size of material that will be trapped.

Normally, sand and stones can be separated using one sieve and sand separated from clay using a much finer sieve.

Lumps of flour can be separated from fine flour or flour separated from sugar in the same way.

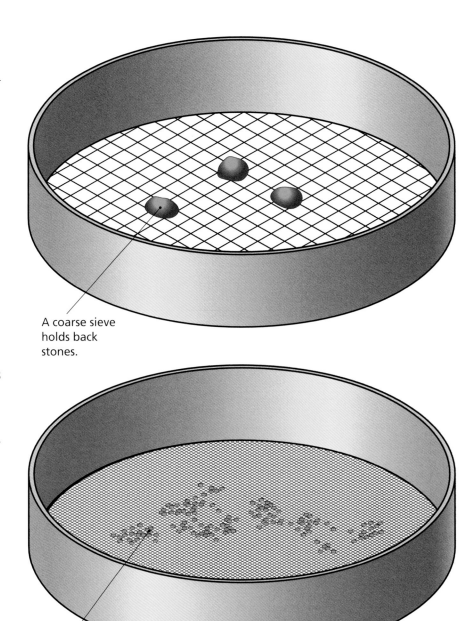

A coarse sieve holds back stones.

A finer sieve holds back sand.

▲ (Picture 1) Sieves are used to separate coarse pieces from fine. These two sieves can separate a soil into three groups: the larger stones are held back on the top sieve, the sand is held back on the second, and the finest material passes through the fine sieve. It could be collected in a dish.

Filtering

A filter is a much finer kind of sieve. Filters are often made of paper. They have holes that are almost too small to see.

A filter is designed to separate an insoluble solid from a liquid containing a dissolved solid. Coffee filters and tea bags are two examples of filtering (Pictures 2 and 3).

▲ (Picture 2) Tea is available in chopped leaves, or as ground leaf in a teabag. The strainer used with tea leaves has bigger holes than the tea bags. Can you figure out why?

Summary

- Some mixtures are hard to separate.
- Different sizes of the same material can be separated by sieving.
- Solids can be separated from liquids by filtering.

▼ (Picture 3) A coffee filter must separate the coffee grains from the dissolved coffee. The holes in the filter paper must be finer than any coffee grain.

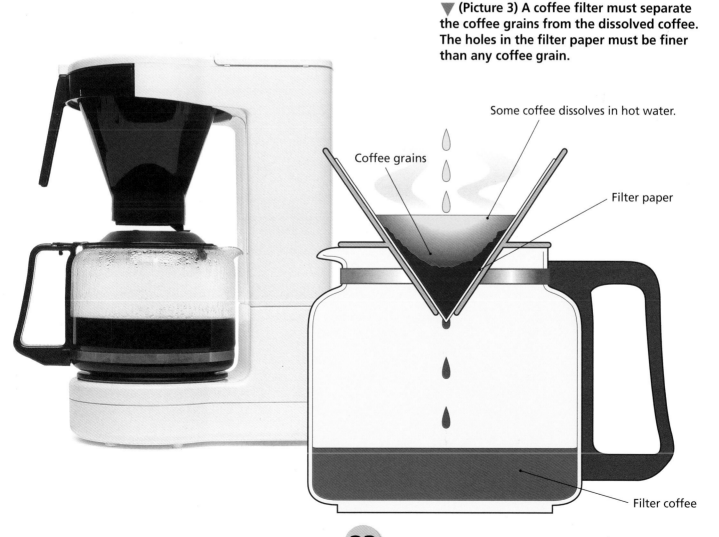

Some coffee dissolves in hot water.

Coffee grains

Filter paper

Filter coffee

Index

Science Matters!

Grolier Educational

First published in the United States in 2003 by Grolier Educational, Sherman Turnpike, Danbury, CT 06816

Copyright © 2003
Atlantic Europe Publishing Company Ltd.

All rights reserved. No part of this publication may be reproduced, stored in a retrieval system, or transmitted in any form or by any means—electronic, mechanical, photocopying, recording, or otherwise—without prior permission of the publisher.

This product is manufactured from sustainable managed forests. For every tree cut down at least one more is planted.

Author
Brian Knapp, BSc, PhD
Educational Consultant
Peter Riley, BSc, C Biol, MI Biol, PGCE
Art Director
Duncan McCrae, BSc
Senior Designer
Adele Humphries, BA, PGCE
Editor
Lisa Magloff, BA
Illustrations
David Woodroffe
Designed and produced by
Earthscape Editions
Reproduced in Malaysia by
Global Color
Printed in Hong Kong by
Wing King Tong Company Ltd
Picture credits
All photographs are from the Earthscape Editions photolibrary, except the following: (c=center t=top b=bottom l=left r=right) USGS cover, 13t.

Library of Congress Cataloging-in-Publication Data
Knapp, Dr. Brian J.
  Science Matters! / [Dr. Brian J. Knapp].
    p. cm.
  Includes index.
  Summary: Presents information on a wide variety of topics in basic biology, chemistry, and physics.
  Contents: v. 1. Food, teeth, and eating—v. 2. Helping plants grow well—v. 3. Properties of materials—v. 4. Rocks and soils—v. 5. Springs and magnets—v. 6. Light and shadows—v. 7. Moving and growing—v. 8. Habitats—v. 9. Keeping warm and cool—v. 10. Solids and liquids—v. 11. Friction—v. 12. Simple electricity—v. 13. Keeping healthy—v. 14. Life cycles—v. 15. Gases around us—v. 16. Changing from solids to liquids to gases—v. 17. Earth and beyond—v. 18. Changing sounds—v. 19. Adapting and surviving—v. 20. Microbes—v. 21. Dissolving—v. 22. Changing materials—v. 23. Forces in action—v. 24. How we see things—v. 25. Changing circuits.
  ISBN 0-7172-5834-3 (set)—ISBN 0-7172-5835-1 (v. 1)—ISBN 0-7172-5836-X (v. 2)—ISBN 0-7172-5837-8 (v. 3)—ISBN 0-7172-5838-6 (v. 4)—ISBN 0-7172-5839-4 (v. 5)—ISBN 0-7172-5840-8 (v. 6)—ISBN 0-7172-5841-6 (v. 7)—ISBN 0-7172-5842-4 (v. 8)—ISBN 0-7172-5843-2 (v. 9)—ISBN 0-7172-5844-0 (v. 10)—ISBN 0-7172-5845-9 (v. 11)—ISBN 0-7172-5846-7 (v. 12)—ISBN 0-7172-5847-5 (v. 13)—ISBN 0-7172-5848-3 (v. 14)—ISBN 0-7172-5849-1 (v. 15)—ISBN 0-7172-5850-5 (v. 16)—ISBN 0-7172-5851-3 (v. 17)—ISBN 0-7172-5852-1 (v. 18)—ISBN 0-7172-5853-X (v. 19)—ISBN 0-7172-5854-8 (v. 20)—ISBN 0-7172-5855-6 (v. 21)—ISBN 0-7172-5856-4 (v. 22)—ISBN 0-7172-5857-2 (v. 23)—ISBN 0-7172-5858-0 (v. 24)—ISBN 0-7172-5859-9 (v. 25)
  1. Science—Juvenile literature. [1. Science.] I. Title.

Q163.K48 2002
500—dc21

2002017302